# ESCAPE THE WOODS

## FOREST HORROR STORIES

### VOLUME 2

Gathered and redrafted

by

**Steven Armstrong**

ESCAPE THE WOODS: FOREST
HORROR STORIES, VOLUME 2

## Note

It is important to remember that most of the following reports are statements from people Steven spoke to via the internet. He has no way of validating whether these claims are factual or imagined. That is up to the reader to decide. In any case, it seems more than apparent that something of high strangeness lurks in the North American wilderness.

## Confidentiality

Many of the following people who shared their stories asked that their real names be kept private. Please respect those willing to share their identities by refraining from harassing them on social media.

## Have You Seen a Cryptid?

If you believe that you have encountered one of these creatures and would like to share your story with the world, shoot me an Email!

bigfoothorrorstories@gmail.com

I would love to check it out! I make an effort to respond to all of my messages.

# Contents

## An Unexplainable Swarm

*There's no question that a small rowboat would be one of the worst places to get attacked by anything, especially when having no idea what the attackers are or where they came from.*

Greetings. My name is Elizabeth, and I'm from Alexandria, Virginia. When I was a teenager, my family rented a cabin on a river in a town called Milboro. The place is up in the mountains and is remarkably beautiful—certainly one of the most scenic locations I've ever visited. Unfortunately, our family trip was cut short by creatures that still terrify me to the core whenever I think about them, and this incident happened well over two decades ago.

While growing up, it was a family tradition to spend about a week in a different rustic area every August before my brother, Eric, and I had to start the school year. Although those vacations contributed to many of my fondest memories, the event in Milboro is by far the worst I can think of. I was only fourteen years old, and I remember feeling that the death of my entire family, including me, was inevitable. But, in a way, I think the experience was somewhat healthy because it helped me not to take my mom, dad, and brother for granted.

It had just reached dusk when my dad decided we should all get in the rowboat and paddle down the calm river to watch the sunset. It was a crystal-clear sky, and he insisted we stay there until the stars lit up the area. I distinctly remember Eric throwing a tantrum because of how hungry he was. My parents regularly joked about how my brother had hanger issues ever since emerging from the womb—something he still deals with to this very day in adulthood.

Everything had started very pleasantly, and I remember feeling thankful that my dad brought us out there even though we were eager for dinner. It easily would've been one of my favorite memories had things not suddenly taken a terrifying turn.

My mom was the first one to mention that she spotted what she at first thought was a glow bug. She made a big deal about it because she had regularly said she hadn't seen many since we arrived in Milboro. She had always had a thing for those insects, often bringing up how she and my aunt loved to gather as many as they could into jars when they were children and then set them free all at once. She said they would refer to that as "nature's light shows," as she and her sister would bring them onto the deck and unleash them for their parents to watch in awe.

She would often joke about how one time my aunt set them free in my grandparents' bedroom, unaware of the hassle that would bring about trying to get them out of the house safely. Those bugs had always been very nostalgic for my mom, and our family would joke about how excited she'd get when we'd encounter them.

Well, I genuinely wish that's all we encountered that night.

It wasn't long until my mom announced she had spotted another one of her favorite creatures, and I distinctly remember the tone of surprise in her voice. I would even go as far as to say it conveyed that she was intimidated. It became clear that she was focused more on our surroundings than the night sky, which is what the rest of us were eyeing. Therefore, we kept missing the glowing organism by the time she tried to point it out to us.

But it was shortly after my mom announced that there were more of them that we all turned to look and saw what looked to be six or seven huge glow bugs about twenty yards from our boat. Something immediately felt off, but I had no idea why. I remember getting an uneasy feeling in the pit of my stomach quickly after seeing them.

"Those things are enormous," my dad commented, his voice hinting at a similar nervous feeling. I think that sensation came partly from the notion that the things were slowly but surely coming closer, and a small rowboat isn't exactly the best place to be crammed into when approached by large, winged pests. I think we all already knew by that point that we weren't among typical glow bugs; these were something else—something that we knew nothing about.

Soon I was startled by the sudden loud sound of my dad clapping his hands. I guess he thought that would deter whatever these things were from coming any closer. But it did nothing to halt their approach. It got to the point where they got so close that my dad started trying to paddle us away, but it was no use; *they* were upon us before we knew it.

I barely had time to acknowledge the somewhat human-like figures of these things. They were probably around eight inches tall, had torsos shaped like ours, legs that reminded me of a grasshopper's, dragonfly-like wings, and little bug-eyed heads. I immediately became so occupied waving my arms around my head to shoo them away that I didn't even notice where all the others had come from. Suddenly, there were so many more of these things swarming around our boat, and they made this awful noise that seemed to vibrate my eardrums. They emanated a frequency that was toxic to our audible senses.

Although my eyes were closed while I tried to protect my head, I could hear my dad's paddle hitting them in midair, causing some creatures to plummet into the surrounding water. I'm sure anyone who's experienced these unexplainable encounters appreciates how quickly it all occurs; the feeling of confusion while simultaneously in fight or flight mode is a remarkably odd state.

When I heard Eric scream, I immediately knew it wasn't just from fear but from pain.

"Get off of him!" my mom and dad yelled simultaneously as the violent commotion escalated. There were moments when I worried that we would capsize the rowboat. I can't imagine how awful it would've been to be in the cold water with those things swarming around us, attempting to keep our heads above the surface while fighting off those creatures.

Eventually, that awful frequency in my ears faded, and soon, the commotion along with it. I remember how we all rapidly breathed while scanning our surroundings, entirely prepared for another attack.

Not only had all the noise faded, but there were no firefly-like glows anywhere in sight. The way they had seemed to vanish into thin air was perhaps the strangest aspect of all. Where would they have gone? If those creatures used nothing but their wings to leave the area, that would have to make them one of the fastest lifeforms on this planet.

I was so freaked out as my dad paddled us back to the dock that I lost the ability to cry. My instincts must've been focused on keeping me alert in case the nasty pests returned. My dad commanded that the three of us rush into the rental house while he tied the boat to the dock, and I felt so grateful to watch him walk through the door shortly after us. If I were in his shoes, I wouldn't have had the courage to remain outside any longer than I had to. The homeowner's boat would've already started drifting downstream the moment we all stepped out of it.

Once inside, I finally saw why my brother screamed while on the river. My mom helped Eric pull up his shirt, and I nearly fainted. Although it wasn't the deepest wound, drops of blood trickled beneath what looked like a small child's bite mark. It looked like impressions from a tiny upper jaw and lower jaw.

Luckily, the blood appeared to have started clotting quickly; however, my parents worried that it could get infected—mainly because we had no idea what those winged creatures were or what toxins might be in their saliva. We were only inside the house for a few minutes before we exited and ran toward our car. Even the few seconds it took us to get to our vehicle were some of the most suspenseful of my life since we couldn't be sure if those winged creatures would appear again.

Because it wasn't busy, we got a doctor to tend to Eric immediately after arriving at the emergency room. The place wasn't hectic, and I'm guessing that's because the area had a relatively small population. They didn't let me inside the room with Eric, so my dad stayed with me in the lobby. I can only wonder what the nurses and doctor thought when they saw the bite mark. They gave him a rabies shot, which he still speaks about as one of the most uncomfortable things he's ever endured. I remember feeling so glad I didn't have to go through anything like that.

It wasn't long before we left the place. Along the drive back to the vacation rental, my parents debated driving home that same night but ultimately concluded we'd be safe if we stayed inside until daylight. The following day, we packed everything up and headed out.

We were pleased that the bite mark healed as quickly as any regular minor wound. It took us a long time to come to grips with what we encountered that evening. Aside from my dad, everyone eventually concluded that those things were fairies. As absurd as that might sound, what else would have the torso and head similar to a human but have wings and legs like an insect? Whatever those things were, I sure hope I never see anything like them again. Though rare, I have found a few stories on the internet where other people claimed to have dealt with something similar.

That terrifying event persuaded me to believe that many creatures of lore are or at least were real entities. Perhaps there just aren't quite as many of them as there once were.

Strange stuff, indeed.

## Biking Through the Mist

*Mountain biking was one of the most effective strategies to clear my head. That was before I nearly lost my life during my last solo excursion.*

The woods used to be my favorite place to clear my head. Nature had always helped me feel so at peace after a week at my demanding job. I work as a financial advisor for wealthy individuals; if you've had any experience doing the same, you're aware of the frequent overwhelming pressure your clients will place on you. Sometimes, it feels as though their future depends entirely on your ability to make well-informed decisions. Honestly, I only do this kind of work because I'm good at analyzing data, and it pays well, but it's definitely not my passion. Anyone who does a job solely because it provides a comfortable living becomes aware that enjoyable hobbies are critical—unless they want to lose their mind. Well, mountain biking used to be the perfect outlet for me, but then came the day I went for a ride that made me feel

incredibly lucky to have gotten home
in one piece.

It happened about five years
ago when I was living and working in
Seattle. Almost every weekend, I
would drive an hour or two outside the
city, searching for new trails that
made me feel alone. As I said,
pedaling vigorously through isolated
locations was the quickest way to strip
the stress away. The absence of noise
from the urban hustle and bustle
worked like magic to refresh my mind
for the upcoming strenuous workweek.
I was a single man back then, so there
was rarely any pushback or plans to
prevent me from engaging in this form
of meditation once the weekend rolled
around. I often miss those

excursions—but that was before I discovered the unexplainable dangers lurking in the woods.

Unless I felt unusually drained from the previous week, I'd always try to head out the door before dawn. Even those drives with far fewer vehicles on the road presented healing qualities. I would almost always make the entire trip without listening to the radio or podcasts, which seemed to help prepare me for Mondays.

I usually tried to avoid popular trails and would often cross paths with less than a handful of other adventurers by getting out there so early. On the day of my frightening experience, I chose a place that someone at a rural gas station recommended. He was a younger man pumping gas at the same time as I, and he noticed the bicycle secured to the rear of my SUV. After stating that he didn't think the place was listed on any smartphone GPS apps, he was kind enough to give me detailed directions to the trailhead. Thinking about that reminds me of how many horror movies have scenes like that.

I wasn't sure whether to trust the stranger's words, but I felt excited as soon as I arrived at the hidden trailhead. It was a misty day, and I assumed it had rained quite the previous night, so I was worried the desolate path might be too sludgy to use. But the course was sheltered by thick tree cover, which helped keep the ground solid enough for a pleasant ride. There weren't any other parked vehicles in sight, which made me even more hopeful that the trail would be in near-perfect condition. If you're a passionate mountain biker, you're probably aware that regular cyclist traffic can mess up an unpaved path in a region like the Pacific Northwest. So, I felt like I got pretty lucky by meeting that gas station patron.

It wasn't long before the relatively flat terrain converted into a steep, winding incline. Though that type could be challenging, I learned to love it for a couple of reasons. Usually, it indicated that I would eventually reach a heavenly view; the other was that the vigorous workout would leave me with a deep sense of satisfaction from having conquered the day.

The deeper I got into the woods, the more it felt like I had entered an Amazonian rainforest, rich with dense, green foliage and all kinds of exotic-sounding birdcalls. Hearing those noises uninterrupted by the busy cityscape was so impactful; it put my mind at ease, even while pedaling for dear life. Well, it wasn't long before the expression "pedaling for dear life" began to feel too literal.

I had been on the trail for about half an hour, and it didn't seem like I was yet near the mountain's peak. Suddenly, I heard a strange galloping-like noise from somewhere directly behind me. I could tell that, whatever was responsible for the sound, had crossed from one side of the trail to the other, for I heard shaking foliage immediately before and after the galloping. But when I looked over my shoulder, there weren't any animals in sight.

I felt slightly uneasy about it because I was confident that it couldn't have been a spooked deer. I had seen way more than enough deer during my journeys to know that they usually sound much lighter on their feet. Whatever this thing was, it sounded significantly bulkier. I wouldn't say I was frightened by the noise, given that I was on my bike, but I still decided it would be wise to keep an eye out if a predator followed my trail. I was mainly concerned that I might've accidentally drawn the curiosity of a mountain lion—a creature known to ambush unsuspecting bikers.

After another few minutes, I began to feel a little more nervous due to arriving at an even steeper incline that drastically slowed my speed. I started moving at a pace that any aggressive animal would be able to outdo with ease. I reached the top without any further signs of anything following me, so I figured that whatever I had heard before wasn't interested in me; they were trying to avoid me.

But after I had parked my bike and admired the vast mountainous landscape, I heard another peculiar noise. It started like a child's laugh but then transitioned into a noise more like a vibration than an audible sound. It had this sort of low-pitched echo at the end of it. I've spent a lot of time thinking about that noise since this occurred, and that's been the only way I can define it.

Something about it made such a lasting impression in my mind. And I've noticed I'll think of the noise whenever I'm over-stressed, even though I'll be dealing with something entirely unrelated. That's always been one of the weirdest parts of this whole thing. I wish I could acquire a scientific explanation for that alone.

Soon after I heard that noise for the first time, I slowly walked toward my bike while looking all around me. As I was about to get on my bike, I saw the creepy white figure standing on the slope that I had used to get to the peak. I had never before seen anything like its pale nude body, and its sunken big black eyes made it so that I couldn't tell what it was looking at. Although its body was angled directly toward me, I sensed it was staring at me from its peripheral vision. It almost seemed like it was trying to act nonchalant like it didn't want me to know that its attention was on me.

Since the figure was relatively human-like, I felt very awkward and wasn't sure whether I should acknowledge it in a friendly way to display that I was peaceful. After a few seconds of not knowing how to react, I silently got back on my bike and pedaled away. Right before heading out of the area, I noticed the figure's neck extended much further than a human's neck could. That was when I knew this wasn't some deranged person in a full-body costume attempting to get a good scare out of me.

Even though the only thing I could think about at the moment was getting as far away from that thing as possible, I noticed how I quickly started to question whether I had imagined the sighting. My brain immediately conformed to attempting to convince me that it was all in my head. I now think that shows how society has conditioned us to reject all things that don't make sense, even when it's right there in plain sight.

At nutty as this might sound to others, I rode about another half of a mile before exhausting myself to the point that I needed to stop for a break. My adrenaline was going too hard, and I pedaled too vigorously to sustain it. I also wanted to pull over to maintain my sanity and prove to myself that nothing was following me. I decided to stop at a clearing more expansive than the previous one. The area was much more open and flatter, so I figured I would have enough warning if that strange white creature were to approach.

I hung out there for a few minutes without any sign the thing was near, so I started to regain a sense of security. Of course, throughout my life, I had heard stories about people seeing things in the woods, so I knew I wasn't alone regarding whatever had happened to me—whether I had truly seen something or not. After enjoying the second view, I returned to my bicycle and resumed my ride at a semi-vigorous speed.

Although things started to feel normal again, I occasionally felt that something was watching me. That intuition continued for another twenty minutes before I heard rustling in the woods to my left. As soon as I checked that direction, I saw the mysterious white figure crawling through the foliage, keeping itself very low to the ground. In addition to how startling the visual was, it terrified me to see the entity creeping along the ground like a mountain lion stalking its prey. As stunned as I was by the scene, I picked up the speed and created a reasonable distance between my follower and me. However, shortly after I made my way around a bend, I observed the white figure cutting through the dense vegetation.

A part of me wanted to scream for help, hoping that at least one other biker was nearby and might respond.

But then I worried that my distress might become a little too evident, thus letting my follower know that I was terrified of it. I knew you should never display signs of weakness; otherwise, you'll risk triggering an undesirable reaction.

The gas station patron informed me that the trail eventually looped around, but he never specified how long it would be before I started making my way back down the mountain. He said I should keep following the path, and I would eventually find myself back at the trailhead. Every minute that passed without reaching the descent elevated my fear. I kept wondering if it could be another hour or two before I started making my way down the mountain, and that made me feel like my stalker would still have multiple opportunities to attack.

It's probably a bit of an exaggeration, but I felt like I almost died from overwhelming relief when I arrived back at my car. And that sensation only amplified after I made it inside and locked the doors. There were a few moments when I considered leaving my bicycle behind. I was reluctant to take the time to secure it to the rear of my vehicle before driving away. Since nobody else was around, I felt the most vulnerable I ever had. It seemed like the perfect time to get attacked while I was distracted with getting everything situated.

I started to feel much better once I advanced a few miles from the trailhead. Although I had no idea what that all-white creature was, I felt confident that it no longer had the chance to get its hands on me. Unfortunately, I wanted to ensure that nothing like that would ever happen again, so I decided to avoid those isolated locations moving forward. It's a damn shame that it scared me that badly, but the last thing I wanted was to be one of those people who vanish in the woods without the case ever getting solved. That potentiality was just too much to endure.

Multiple others have suggested that what I saw that day was a cryptid referred to as *the rake*. I've read everything I can get my hands on about that creature, and I suppose there are similarities; however, I haven't yet found any reports of the rake being all white like the thing I saw that day. I guess there's always the chance that the creature could have had some health defect that altered the pigment of its skin. My teenage nephew insists that it must have been an alien.

Although the creature did appear somewhat intelligent, it seemed a little too primitive to be capable of something like intergalactic travel. It's just too hard for me to imagine anything that acted so animalistic to know how to operate advanced technology. I believe aliens are among us, but I don't see any reason they'd want to reveal themselves to us. I think that whatever I saw that day was a member of a species that occupies our wilderness, but there are too few to gather reliable scientific data. If anyone has detailed information on those creatures, please send a message to Steven Armstrong as soon as possible. I would love nothing more than to hear what you have to say. I've heard several times that it can be very comforting to find others who can relate to you regarding these mysterious sightings.

Thank you for giving me a place to share my story. I plan to keep reading these books for as long as you publish them.

## The Backyard Shapeshifter

*A backyard is usually an excellent place for a child's first camping trip, as it can help acclimate them to the outdoor world. But what happens if a stranger visits them in the middle of the night?*

Hey, I'm Tia, and I'm from Carbondale, Colorado, which is also where my chilling story occurred. Because of what I went through, I don't allow my children to tent camp in our backyard. It makes me sad that I have to be strict about that, but I haven't been able to trust the woods ever since I discovered that unexplainable entities exist.

I was once very close with a girl named Sally. I thought of her as the perfect friend; she was pretty, upbeat, and loved everything involving nature. We were only ten years old when she convinced her father to set up their tent for us in their backyard. If I remember correctly, her family was preparing for a camping trip that upcoming weekend, and I suppose she was too excited to wait a few more days before she could sleep outside.

Although Sally had been on camping trips in the past, she had never camped in a tent. Her family owned an RV and used it several times to travel across the country, but it felt like sleeping inside a small house. The family decided to do something a little more rustic for their upcoming camping excursion. Perhaps it wasn't until then that Sally's parents had decided she was old enough and mature enough to handle being out in a tent for the duration of the night. They probably thought she would get too creeped out by the sounds of scavenging animals, so they held off until she was a bit older and would understand there was no such thing as monsters in the woods. Well, it's a shame that she and I had to learn there is, in fact, something much more frightening than black bears out there.

Sally's family had a spacious backyard, so, in theory, it should've been an excellent location to familiarize ourselves with tent camping. I remember rushing with her to the tent right after dinner and immediately started gossiping about our classmates. Since it was summer, we talked about what the cutest boys had been up to since the school year ended. Sally was a lot less shy around boys than I was at that age, so I recall feeling very entertained by her filling me in on the details of what they were up to. Her older brother worked as a lifeguard at a local pool, and she spent most of her afternoons there—the most popular hangout spot for boys and girls around our age.

It was right around the time that Sally had revealed a surprising crush that we were confronted by a second, much more alarming surprise. The combination of multiple flashlights and electronic lanterns enabled us to see silhouettes of anyone or anything approaching the tent, but what we observed made it difficult to distinguish whether it was man or animal. At first, I assumed it was some kind of creature because it appeared to be moving on four feet and looked significantly smaller than a child. We couldn't tell if it grew before our eyes or rushed toward the tent at remarkable speed, creating the illusion that it was growing taller.

Neither of us heard the footsteps; if the thing had been silent while moving about the ground, it would've helped the impression that it was increasing in size. Also, I recall how the environment seemed to go entirely quiet soon before the silhouette appeared. The whole thing was so mysterious and occurred before I had any idea that monsters existed.

Although we both managed to remain quiet, I think it's safe to assume we would've screamed our little hearts out had we not felt so disturbed. The creepy figure appeared to leave the scene seconds after appearing, but Sally and I stayed quiet, hoping it was gone for good. Well, it wasn't. Only moments later, it reappeared. But this time, when it neared the tent, it made a strange sniffing noise. The sounds of those sniffs indicated that this was indeed an animal, though it was tough to figure out what kind. All we knew was that it was considerably larger than Sally and I combined. At one point, it looked like the intruder grew something out of its head shaped like rabbit ears—which occurred immediately before the silhouette appeared to shrink again. I can't even begin to express how oddly it moved.

Nothing about its motions resembled movement from anything I had ever seen before. It was almost like watching an old silent film with many damaged frames, making it look like the characters were skipping from one place to the next.

There were quite a few instances where Sally or I could've unzipped the tent's window screen and gotten a good look at the intruder, but we were both too frightened by the response that might bring about. The other terrifying aspect was that we couldn't know whether the intruder knew we were in there. I figured it must've heard us gossiping earlier, which was probably why it snooped around in the first place, but then I wondered if it was merely attracted by the glow radiating from inside the tent.

Without Sally's permission, I turned off the flashlight and the electric lantern before she could protest. That was when we started hearing bizarre noises. It sounded a lot like a human's cackle, but the strange part was how I couldn't get a handle on whether it was a male or female voice. Frankly, it seemed to fluctuate between the two. Hearing those noises left us with even more questions. Not only were we wondering why the intruder had shown up in the first place, but what did it want with us? Why did it repeatedly approach our tent?

Soon, the cackles seemed to circle us at an incredible speed. The terror quickly escalated to the point where neither of us could take it anymore. Simultaneously, we screamed as loud as we could, and it wasn't long before we heard Sally's father calling out to us as he approached. But before he even made it over to us, he started hollering at someone or something else. "Hey!" he called out. "Who are you? What are you doing on my land?"

There was something about hearing him acknowledge the intruder that instantly made things feel even more real. I wanted to believe it was nothing more than a horrible dream. But Sally's father's startled reaction made it known it was anything but. Soon, it sounded like her dad ran in another direction, following the intruder.

A bit later, my heart nearly jumped out of my chest when we suddenly heard Sally's father's voice only feet away from our tent. Fortunately, the man sounded unharmed but out of breath. As we stepped out of the tent, he asked us if we had seen that thing. I thought it was creepy to hear him say that he didn't even know whether it was a man or an animal. He said it was too dark even to tell if it was a man or woman while in a more human-like form. In any case, he was disturbed by the sighting and rushed us inside the house. Sally's father kept looking around as we walked through their dark backyard. It was apparent that he felt threatened by the intruder, which freaked me out even more. Sally's father wasn't a small guy, so it felt weird to see him that scared. It made him seem childlike, in a way.

Sally's mother immediately called the police as soon as her father informed her of what had happened. I remember him saying something about how he needed to ensure the kidnapper never came around again. The word kidnapper made the whole thing even more frightening because Sally's father interpreted the intruder as a serious threat. I was so glad he came out there when he did;

otherwise, who knows what might have happened to us?

The police officers got to work as soon as they arrived. They spent the next thirty minutes searching for the trespasser but failed to come up with anything. They even had difficulty locating tracks that might've belonged to another human. And they should've been able to find something of the sort because I remember them talking about how the soil was soft due to a recent storm.

It wasn't until after the police left that we overheard Sally's parents discussing what her father had seen. He told his wife that he had seen a strange-looking person wearing an even stranger-looking outfit comprised of animal skins. Additionally, he saw what looked to be rabbit ears atop their head. He thought he was losing his mind as he watched the ears shrink until they were no longer visible. It was easy to tell that he was very disturbed and desperate for reassurance that he hadn't gone insane.

Everything he told Sally's mother matched perfectly with the silhouette we saw multiple times from inside the tent—which was alarming. I wished he had said he saw a homeless man running away from the property. Even though that would've also been frightening, the idea that we had encountered something possibly half human and half animal made everything far more terrifying.

Although it will probably remain unclear for the remainder of my life, I'm confident we encountered a skinwalker that night. For many years, I tried to convince myself it was a ridiculous theory, but after reading so many books full of strange encounters, I realized there is so much more in our woods than science declares. It genuinely feels like a disservice to humanity how the authorities don't warn us that we can encounter things in our forests that aren't widely talked about. It makes me sad to think how some parents are entirely unaware of the danger they're putting their children in by allowing them to roam free in their woodland backyards. No matter how hard they fought me, I would never let my kids do such a thing.

What would have happened had that creepy trespasser gotten their hands on Sally and me? I highly doubt we would have ever been seen again. Please be careful while enjoying our beautiful outdoor environments. They're not as safe as most of us like to believe.

Thanks a million for taking the time to read my submission; it was noticeably therapeutic to write all of this down. I hope it encourages others to share their unexplainable and mysterious stories. I think it's lovely that we're forming a community so accepting of these strange happenings. These publications needed to happen long ago, so I'm glad they're gaining popularity. I'll send another report if I ever go through something weird again.

## The Woman of the Pond

*It's remarkable how some people see strange entities so close to their properties, leaving them wondering when they might try to get inside their homes.*

I would rather not disclose my name or the location of where my experience took place, for I still have family in the area, and I don't think they'd appreciate paranormal investigators snooping around there. I realize there's a slim chance of that happening, but I would still rather avoid any chance of that happening. I hope you understand.

I was fifteen when my family moved us into a new house in Massachusetts. They had worked hard for many years, saving what they perceived to be appropriate savings to provide enough cushion while building their own business.

One of my favorite parts about our land was that we had a private pond. It wasn't any small watering hole; it was big enough to paddle around in a rowboat without worrying about getting caught in aquatic vegetation. There was an antique rowboat at the edge of the shore, which gave my parents the idea to get a brand-new one as a housewarming gift. I remember getting so excited by the idea of reading novels inside that thing during good weather. I had been an avid reader since I was a small child and was always looking for new cozy places to enjoy my books. I also had dreams of being an author one day, so I planned on bringing a notebook into the boat on occasion.

When we first moved there, everything seemed fantastic. It felt like a perfect move following the death of our pet cat that we loved dearly. Our family needed something to be excited about, and moving to that house seemed to fulfill that need.

Shortly after getting the new boat, we headed to the nearest rescue shelter to get a new cat. At first, we had told ourselves that we couldn't imagine getting another pet, as we wanted to avoid future heartbreak. But, as many pet owners experience, the void becomes too powerful, and you find yourself longing for any way to fix that. We ended up finding a beautiful black and white kitten that was about five months old. One of the other cats at the shelter had recently given birth to a litter, so we decided to take one of the babies home, hoping it would have a nice long life with us in our new house. My dad didn't particularly care for the name, but he allowed Mom and I to have our way by naming our new kitten "Muffins."

Since our previous cat, Manny, was a housecat his whole life, we wanted to do something different this time and allow Muffins to be an outdoor cat. So, we stopped to get him a harness and a leash on our way home from the shelter.

There was something very satisfying for our family about walking that cat around our new property. It was a very wholesome thought to know that we were familiarizing ourselves with the place as a family. I remember having some of our best family talks while walking around there. There's no question that it strengthened our bond. And we loved watching the curious kitty explore nature for the first time. I'll never forget how he pranced around in the grass, going after butterflies, grasshoppers, and dandelions. He was such a goofball, and I immediately loved him with all my heart. That's why finding him dead near the pond's edge was incredibly difficult.

To say that our family was stunned would be an understatement. The sorrow of losing our new family member and the mystery of how he even got outside in the middle of the night was too much to take in. Muffins had been alternating between sleeping in my and my parents' rooms. We kept our doors closed, so it made no sense how he could've gotten out of the house. Muffins slept with my parents on the night of his death, so I couldn't verify whether my mom or dad walked out of their room at night and neglected to shut the door.

My dad scaled the place in search of openings that he could've squeezed through but was never able to locate any potential escape routes. On top of that, Muffins was an unusually clingy kitten; he never wanted to leave his nearest human. We couldn't tell whether he was remarkably affectionate or afraid of abandonment. It was amazing how quickly that death brought a powerful gloominess to our new living situation—one that we seemed incapable of shaking.

That situation placed so much tension over all three of us, leading toward the first time I had very ugly arguments with my parents. Even though I knew they were responsible people, I couldn't let go of the suspicion that they had messed up by leaving their bedroom door open. What's even crazier is that Muffins still would've had to get past another door even if he had found a way out of their bedroom. I think we all wanted to blame someone just to get an answer as to how the tragedy could've occurred. I couldn't accept the reality that such a cute and innocent little soul had left us that early on.

My dad was the only one who went near the lifeless kitty, and it wasn't until a few days after the event that he revealed it appeared that something had wrung his neck. He told me he didn't want to bring it up at first because he worried that that suspicion would make me too afraid to stay in our new house any longer. I believe he also wanted to dismiss that possibility because it still didn't make sense, and he didn't want to give himself an unrealistic reason to be on high alert.

Our move to that house was supposed to be a very positive thing, so he was doing everything in his power to avoid changing that energy. Of course, the kitten's sudden death had already placed an enormous damper on our new living situation; therefore, talk of a murderous intruder would have taken the already grim feelings to new heights. Understandably, both of my parents wanted us to refrain from rushing to any extreme conclusions, especially if the chances of us ever getting to the bottom of it were slim.

But eventually, the tension within our household got so bad that my dad decided he had to do anything that might help calm things down. A week or two after the event, my dad came home with another cat from the shelter. He went there intending to get another kitten but ended up settling for a cat that the staff said was probably just over a year old. At first, Mom wasn't thrilled about the gift, for she didn't want something else to worry about, but all three of us quickly fell in love with it. It's a bit of a cliche name, but we ended up calling him Mittens because it was similar to Muffins, and I guess we looked at it like it was a way to honor our deceased kitten.

We started the same routine with Mittens, walking him all over the property and getting acquainted with our land. He was a bit jumpier than Muffins, which led us to believe that he might've had some traumatic experiences before getting picked up by the shelter. Because of that, we tried to take extra good care of him, making sure to be considerate of how much physical interaction we gave him while he was still getting to know us. We were extremely cautious to avoid accidentally creating abrupt noises that might startle him.

Only a few days later, Mittens turned up dead. I was the first to find him near the shrubs in front of our house. I have a hard time talking about it because it instantly reminds me how his back and all four legs were bent in strange directions. We knew this couldn't have been a predator, as there were no signs of anything having tried to consume him.

Dad suggested that he must've fallen out a window, but he hadn't considered how the house was only two stories. To me, the potential plummet didn't seem high enough to kill a cat and definitely not high enough to inflict that level of visible damage.

After that horrible situation, the three of us agreed not to get another cat or pet, at least in the foreseeable future. That second death triggered us to do everything we could to close ourselves off from sorrow. We were so desperate to see our new living situation as a positive change in our lives that we did all we could to disregard any sad feelings. My parents repeatedly told me that we had to stay positive no matter what dark thoughts crept into our minds.

Because of the initiative to force optimism, we started implementing activities around the property that would make us feel good and enable positive distractions. We started doing a lot of picnics, bringing a few blankets to a different spot on our land each time.

One night, after picnicking, we decided that the weather was too perfect to go inside, so we headed for the rowboat. My parents had had quite a bit of wine, so they felt more adventurous than usual. While walking toward the pond, we all paused our strides when we saw someone standing near the water. Quickly switching into protective mode, my dad started running toward the pond without saying anything. Right away, I knew he thought that the mysterious individual was responsible for the death of our pets. He was the type of guy who was usually very calm until something pushed him over the edge, and this was one of those moments. My mom and I both wanted to stop him, but we knew it was no use.

Unsure of what to do, Mom and I dropped our belongings and jogged after Dad. Although we didn't want to participate in the altercation, we didn't want him to deal with everything alone. It wasn't long before we saw the trespassing individual was a female. I'm not sure why I initially assumed it was a man, for they had long hair and a body that was extremely thin and appeared malnourished. I remember how the horrible feeling in my stomach worsened with every step we took toward the pond. But I figured it was just from anxiety over the idea that there was likely about to be a fight.

Some of me wanted to avoid an altercation, but I also wanted vengeance for our cats. I felt so disgusted by the possibility that they had been murdered that I would have traded pretty much anything to catch whoever or whatever committed the crimes.

I couldn't believe it when I saw my dad turn away once he got closer to the intruder. It was tough to imagine him running from anyone, especially someone appearing as thin and weak as this particular individual. After running a few steps toward us, he started shouting for us to stay away. "Don't come any closer!" he said. "Go back to the house!"

Mom and I were so confused, and that feeling only increased when we watched the thin intruder tackle my dad. "We have to help him!" I yelled as I resumed running toward the scene, but Mom grabbed my arm and stopped me from getting closer. She ran me toward the house, but I struggled to set myself free when I looked over my shoulder. The skinny woman was on top of my dad, scratching his face. It didn't make sense how he couldn't push the woman off him. She was clearly a lot smaller than him, so how could she possibly be any stronger?

After setting myself free from my mom's grip, I ran toward him again but ultimately stumbled and fell, giving my mom enough time to catch up to me. As she was helping me to my feet, I saw the intruder's black eyes. Even though I was still a good distance away, I immediately picked up on what felt like demonic energy, and I could tell Mom did as well. "We have to get inside and call for help," she said.

"But what if they don't get here in time?" I asked, becoming more hysterical by the second.

"There's nothing we can do to help your father," Mom said. "We need to get to a phone right away!"

I considered trying to break free again but ultimately concluded that she had the right advice. I could tell I wouldn't be any match for the intruder, given that my dad was already having trouble defending himself. I would probably only get in the way and risk either of us, if not both of us, getting killed.

I ran upstairs as soon as we made it inside, rushing toward the window that provided a view of the pond. As soon as I looked through the glass, I saw the weirdest part yet; the slender woman was hovering above the pond water. I was so distracted by that strange sight that it took me a while to notice Dad was crawling away. Further panic set in as soon as I saw his clothes were bloody from all the scratches he had just endured. I watched him try to get up, and that was when the slender intruder turned around and hovered back toward him.

"No!" I yelled as she got back on top of him and sunk her nails into his torso. It was so bizarre watching the scrawny figure manhandle my dad. My father wasn't any ordinary shrimp; he was a burly guy with impressive strength, and I'm not sure, but I'm guessing he had to be over 200 pounds. So, to see this individual, who couldn't have weighed any more than

100 pounds, completely overpower him, was remarkably disturbing.

As I watched the carnage continue from behind the window, I repeatedly yelled to my mom that we had to do something before dad got killed. While my mom told me to shut up so that she could speak to the 911 operator, I watched the intruder drag my dad by his collar toward the pond.

"Oh no, she's about to drown him!" I yelled loud enough to get my mom off the phone and run outside. I immediately followed her lead, preparing for a violent altercation. My adrenaline had never pumped so hard in my life, and I was ready in every way to protect my family. I might have been young and naive, but I wouldn't go down without a fight.

The scrawny individual was already at the water's edge by the time we were halfway to the pond. "We have to hurry!" I kept yelling to my mom, hoping it would get the two of us to the scene sooner.

After I had made my way within feet of the scrawny woman, she screeched and hovered away from me until she floated above the water. I was so confused by everything, including my dad's beaten body, the intruder floating above the water, and the fact that she ran away from me as soon as I neared her but not my father, who was at least three times the size of me.

The scrawny intruder screeched at me while mom and I tried to help Dad to his feet. Something about the way she looked at me made me feel that she was frightened by my presence. But it just didn't make sense how she could be intimidated by me but not my father. I kept thinking it would be any moment before she rushed over to us and sunk her nails into my or Mom's flesh, but she stayed put.

The intruder kept screaming like a demon out of hell throughout our walk back to the house. I almost couldn't believe it when we made it back inside without the creepy intruder approaching us. The screams had faded entirely by the time a police officer pulled into our driveway and rang the doorbell. I glanced out the window once more as my mother let the officer inside and noticed that the trespasser was nowhere in view.

The police officer appeared on the verge of fainting after getting a look at my dad. I could tell he was very confused by our story. He repeatedly asked if we were sure whether it was an unarmed female who attacked. And, for whatever reason, he continued to disregard the part about the intruder hovering above the water. I could tell that several statements didn't sit well with the authority figure. As frustrating as it was, I can't say I wouldn't act any differently had I been in his shoes. I still had trouble believing my own perceptions of the whole thing.

Both my mom and the police officer wanted to bring my dad to the hospital, but he continued to insist that it wasn't necessary. He looked pretty banged up to me, but I now understand why he probably wanted to avoid the cost of something like that. I was naive to think anyone could go to the hospital anytime and not fear getting into overwhelming debt. I can even remember my dad getting so upset while arguing with the two of them about it, attempting to make himself appear less injured than he was.

The officer spent considerable time searching the premises with one of his colleagues, but neither found evidence of anyone having been there other than my dad's injuries. Before they left, the officer in charge told us that he had never before dealt with anything like it and provided us with his personal phone number to call in case the culprit showed up again.

Nobody in our family knew what to do after the police left. We were all stumped, and it wasn't easy to imagine going outside in the near future. My parents instructed me not to go outside without them for any reason whatsoever. I hated the recent incident for so many reasons. Not only had my dad been brutally beaten, but I couldn't even enjoy the pond with the new boat. Everything felt ruined, and it was challenging to imagine things returning to normal anytime soon—if ever.

My mom tried to cheer my dad and me up with various board games. I admired her determination to hold herself together, but her pretend enthusiasm wasn't effective. Everything felt so gloomy and scary compared to when we first moved into that new house.

I'll never forget when Mom screamed out of nowhere while we played Yahtzee in the den that night. She almost fell out of her seat, and when I turned around, I nearly did as well. Seeing that raggedy, malnourished-looking woman glide down the stairway and shriek at us was almost too much for my heart to bear. And the most frightening aspect was observing how my parents didn't know how to react to the repeat intruder. Understandably, they were still having trouble accepting any of it as real.

Out of sheer desperation to protect my family, I stepped toward the decrepit-looking intruder, shouting at her to leave us alone. As soon as I got closer, she hissed in a way that indicated she was afraid. It was like how she had reacted when my mom and I approached her near the pond. I glanced at my parents; they looked even more surprised than I was. On top of that, she had a weird look of surprise—like she wondered why my family was there. Suddenly, it became clear that we were dealing with a ghost.

I'm sure some readers will wonder how we hadn't already reached that conclusion; none of us believed in ghosts in the first place, and we especially didn't believe in them having the ability to harm a living person with their bare hands. And as stupid as it sounds, both of my parents insisted that she couldn't have glided above the water earlier; they said the water had to have been shallow enough to create the illusion that she was. Of course, everything was so hectic while it was happening that none of us got a good look at many details. We were too busy trying to survive.

With a slight sense of newfound confidence, I decided to take another step. Again, the creepy intruder seemed intimidated. Additionally, it appeared that she was weakening by the second. It seemed like she couldn't escape even if she wanted to. That was when Mom brought something to my attention—I was wearing the cross necklace handed down throughout the generations. My mom got it from my grandma, who then passed it to me. She gave it to me quite a bit earlier than she had planned, for I often talked about it when I was a small child.

It wasn't any typical cross necklace, but one covered with colored jewels that created all sorts of beautiful reflections from sunlight. I had always thought the thing was mesmerizing, but my mom didn't wear it as often as she liked because she thought it was a tad heavy and uncomfortable. She appreciated the family heirloom but usually left it in her jewelry box until it was time to visit Grandma.

"The cross repels her," Mom said. I glanced at Dad; his gaze conveyed that he was thinking the same thing. Suddenly, it felt as though the tables had turned. It seemed that I had the upper hand and was now the one instilling the terror.

I took a few more steps toward the creepy woman while holding the cross necklace in front of me. The intruder's eyes went wider than I thought possible, reiterating that they were anything but a regular human. The closer I got, the quicker she backed away. She eventually collapsed onto the staircase, putting her hand out in front of her, begging me not to come any closer. I felt no sympathy, given what she had done to my dad. I kept moving forward until the cross was inches away from her forehead.

Out of nowhere, she vanished. What's strange is that my family and I don't even remember her fading away or leaving; I can't emphasize enough how, one moment, she was there, and the next, she was gone. Then we noticed that the nearest door was ajar; not one of us remembers seeing it open. However, it was immediately noticeable that the environment felt much better. I don't know how to put it other than to say tension had disappeared.

My parents and I hadn't noticed how much weight had been resting on our shoulders until that point. It's not like we hadn't acknowledged how down we all were after the multitude of grim incidents, but I suppose the tension had been building steady enough for us not to realize just how bad it had gotten. We all agreed that there was an undeniable newfound sense of peace; somehow, we knew it would last. We conquered the negativity that had entered our lives.

Our family became much more religious after that incident, for we suspected we wouldn't have survived had it not been for one of us wearing that cross necklace. That notion attached new meaning to almost everything in our lives, and we found it even easier to feel immense gratitude for all we had. As we had immediately expected, following the incident inside the house, the creepy woman never returned. We even got another cat and then a dog, and both went on to live long, healthy lives. It was lovely to feel the energy of the property return to what it should've felt right after we moved there. It felt like we had an opportunity to make up for the recent horror. I no longer doubt that negative entities can linger around properties and turn them into miserable spaces, no matter how beautiful and welcoming the lands might appear from the outside.

My parents still live in that

house, and I visit them frequently.

Life has been very good for us.

## More *Escape the Woods*

Don't forget to read *Escape the Woods: Forest Horror Stories, Volume 3.*

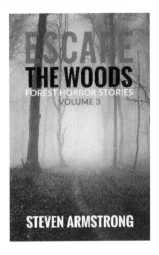

## Bonus Report

To unlock the bonus report, *A Fawn in the Fence*, all you need to do is subscribe to my FREE newsletter. You'll then instantly receive an email containing the document. It happens to be one of my favorite stories.

Visit this link to Get it Now:

https://bit.ly/3r3wNWg

## Submit a Review

Thank you so much for purchasing this book. If you could find the time to post a short review where you purchased the book, it would boost its visibility to new readers. The more readers I acquire, the more time I can put toward gathering sasquatch reports and publishing new books.

## Shoot Me an Email

If you would like to contact me, send me an Email. I'll try my best to respond to your message promptly.

My Email address is:

BigfootHorrorStories@gmail.com

## Instagram

Another fun way to stay in touch is if you follow the official *Bigfoot Horror Stories* Instagram account. I regularly post sasquatch-related content and do my best to reply to all messages and comments.

My Instagram username is:

@BigfootHorrorStories

## About the Author

Steven Armstrong grew up in and around the cloudy but beautiful city of Tacoma, Washington. He's had a powerful passion for the subject ever since he watched a bigfoot-related documentary with his grandfather at the age of eight.

Having always been an avid reader and writer, it eventually dawned on Steven that he could combine all three of his hobbies and even create something that many others could appreciate and learn from. After spending a good amount of time chatting with someone who claimed to have had a sasquatch encounter, Steven attempted to put the story down onto paper, thus, birthing his project, *Bigfoot Horror Stories.*